AMERICA IN WORLD WAR II

1941

AMERICA
IN WORLD
WAR II

EDWARD F. DOLAN

THE MILLBROOK PRESS
BROOKFIELD, CONNECTICUT

Maps by Joe Le Monnier

Cover photograph courtesy of the National Archives

Photographs courtesy of: the National Archives:
pp. 8, 10, 13, 15, 19, 23, 24 (top), 26, 31, 48,
54, 55, 64; AP/Wide World Photos: pp. 24 (bottom), 37, 58; UPI/Bettmann Newsphotos: pp. 34,
35, 41; Horace Bristol, Life Magazine © Time
Warner Inc.: pp. 47 (painting by Kohei Ezaki),
53 (painting by Chosei Miwa); The Bettmann Ar-
chive: p. 61; Library of Congress: p. 63.

Cataloging-in-Publication Data

Dolan, Edward F., 1924–

America in World War II: 1941 / Edward F. Dolan
p.   cm.
Bibliography: p.
Includes index
1. World War, 1939–1945—United States
—Juvenile literature.
I. Title   II. Series
940.5373
ISBN: 0-395-65944-2 (pbk.)

CONTENTS

AMERICA IN WORLD WAR II

1941

ONE: DECEMBER 7, 1941

The thunder of aircraft engines filled the dawn air. It echoed across an area of the Pacific Ocean 275 miles north of the Hawaiian islands as plane after plane took off from the flight decks of the aircraft carriers of the Japanese Navy's First Air Fleet. The planes, 183 bombers and fighters in all—gathered in a giant formation above the fleet and turned southward. The day was a cold and windswept Sunday. The time was 6:20 A.M., December 7, 1941.

Flying at the head of the formation was Lieutenant Commander Mitsuo Fuchida. He glanced down at the fleet far below him. Riding through rough waves that sent mountains of water crashing across the decks were ships of all sizes. He could make out six carriers, two battleships, two heavy cruisers, and eleven destroyers. Pitching wildly about them were fifteen smaller vessels.

A feeling of pride surged through the flier. After fighting heavy seas all the way from Japan, the mighty fleet had arrived here yesterday for the purpose of launching a surprise attack against the U.S. naval and air forces in the Hawaiian islands. Fuchida had been given the honor of leading the first wave of that attack. The planes of the second wave were

Japanese planes prepare to take off from their Japanese Navy carrier on December 7, 1941.

now being moved into position on the carrier decks and would take off just after 7 A.M. In all, the two waves would consist of 366 planes.

Fuchida also knew that other Japanese forces were in the Pacific this morning. They were hundreds of miles over the gray horizon. As he was staging his attack, they would move against the military units stationed on four U.S. possessions—the Philippine islands near the east coast of Asia and the small islands of Midway, Wake, and Guam far out in the Pacific.

The United States would not be alone in feeling the harsh touch of Japanese might. Also due for attack were two British possessions. One was the island of Hong Kong, which stood just off the coast of China. The other lay far to the south of China. Located in Southeast Asia, it was the peninsula country of Malaya. Further, Malaya's neighbor, the independent nation of Siam (today called Thailand), was to be invaded.

GEN. HIDEKI TOJO

General Tojo was the premier of Japan at the time of Pearl Harbor. He and his supporters were greatly in favor of waging war against the United States. They were opposed by many Japanese officials—among them Admiral Yamamoto and former Prime Minister Fuminaro Konoye—who thought that such a war could not be won. General Tojo pushed aside their objections and called for the December 7 attack.

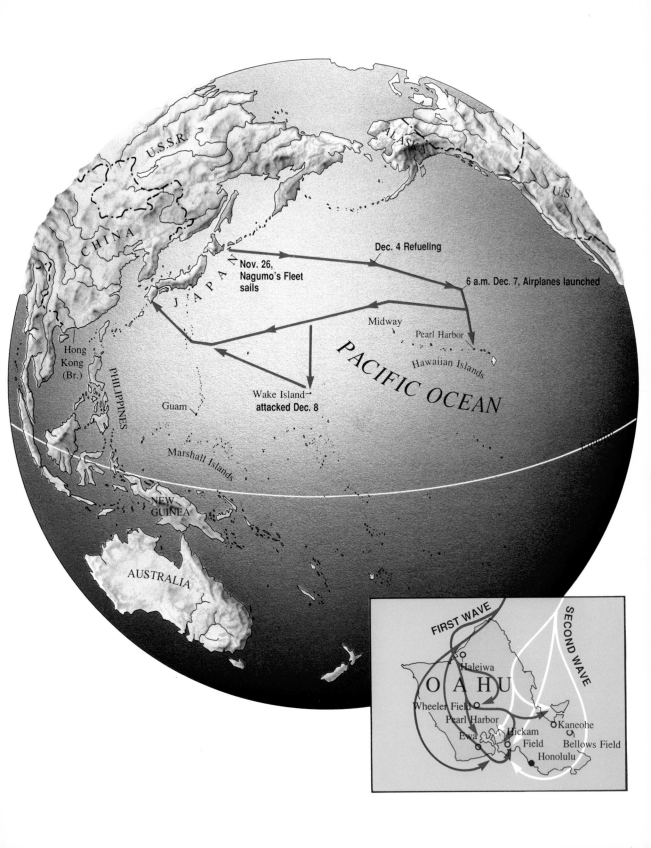

Nov. 26,
Nagumo's Fleet
sails

Dec. 4 Refueling

6 a.m. Dec. 7, Airplanes launched

U.S.S.R.

ALASKA

U.S.

CHINA

J A P A N

Hong
Kong
(Br.)

PHILIPPINES

Guam

Wake Island
attacked Dec. 8

Midway

Pearl Harbor

Hawaiian Islands

PACIFIC OCEAN

Marshall Islands

NEW
GUINEA

AUSTRALIA

FIRST WAVE

SECOND WAVE

O A H U

Haleiwa

Wheeler Field

Pearl Harbor

Ewa

Hickam
Field

Kaneohe

Bellows Field

Honolulu

For many years Japan had sought to become the dominant power in East and Southeast Asia. Today's attacks would pave the way for Japan to achieve an important goal—the seizure of lands at the very foot of Southeast Asia. They were lands rich in natural resources—oil and metals among them—that Japan badly needed to keep its military machine fueled as the quest for domination continued.

But two powerful nations, the United States and Great Britain, stood in the way. They would surely try to stop the invasion. The purpose of this day's attacks was to eliminate or weaken their resolve by crippling their armies, fighting ships, and planes.

Fuchida turned his gaze southward. An empty sea stretched away to the horizon. His target lay 275 miles away. It was the island of Oahu, where most of the U.S. naval and air bases in Hawaii were clustered. If all went well, the bombers and fighters in his wave would swoop down on Oahu in just an hour and a half.

If all went well . . .

The Japanese commander hoped that his planes would not be spotted before they reached their destination or be detected by the five U.S. Army radar stations on Oahu until the very last moment. At that time it would be too late for the Americans to fight back.

CAUGHT BY SURPRISE · The sun came out as Fuchida's wave neared its destination. But, for long minutes, a thick blanket of clouds covered the Hawaiian islands. Then, right on schedule at 7:40 A.M., the clouds broke and the northern shore of Oahu came into view. Fuchida led the way down the island's eastern side. Then he banked west, flew along the southern coast, and swept past the city of Honolulu.

A photo taken from a Japanese plane during its approach to Pearl Harbor on the morning of the attack.

Fuchida was delighted. All seemed quiet and peaceful over on the shore. No puffs of exploding anti-aircraft shells came up to greet him. Nor did he glimpse a single U.S. plane streaking into the air. He was certain that he had caught the Americans completely unawares.

Actually, Fuchida's approach *had* been detected. At about 7 o'clock, while his planes were still some 130 miles out at sea, the Army radar station on the northern coast of Oahu suddenly showed a number of blips on its screen. The two soldiers there notified a superior officer of what they were seeing. But the officer was not worried by their report and said that the blips were probably caused by some U.S. bombers that were due to arrive from California that morning. Nothing more was done about the telltale blips.

The early-morning risers of Honolulu were enjoying the start of a quiet Sunday as Fuchida's wave drew near the city. Some were eating breakfast. Some were on their way to church. Some were out for a stroll along Waikiki Beach. They all heard the drone of engines and saw the planes filling the distant sky like a giant swarm of bees. And they all thought the same thing—that they were seeing some sort of military training exercise.

Many people were still asleep. On hearing the planes, they came groggily awake for a moment. Then, also thinking that they were hearing an air exercise, they rolled over and went back to sleep.

Moments later, there was a horrified cry in the streets and along Waikiki Beach. Some of the planes were so close that the markings on their wings and fuselages were clearly visible. Those markings were not the stars used by the United States. Instead, each ship bore a flaming red circle—the symbol of the Rising Sun. It could mean but one thing. This was no military exercise! This was a Japanese attack!

ATTACK! ATTACK! ATTACK! While he was still sweeping toward Honolulu, Lieutenant Commander Fuchida radioed an order to his pilots: *"To! To! To!"*

The words were the beginning syllables of the Japanese word *totugekiseyo,* meaning to "charge" or "attack." The order was given at 7:47 A.M.

Instantly, the formation began to break up. Groups of bombers and fighters fanned out in different directions and roared toward specific targets. In all, there were to be six targets. Five were airfields located at various points on Oahu. The sixth was the most important target of all—the U.S. Navy's giant base at Pearl Harbor.

Pearl Harbor was located a little less than 10 miles east of downtown Honolulu. Entered through a wide channel, it is one of the finest natural ports in the world. It boasts 10

ADM. ISOROKU YAMAMOTO

Admiral Yamamoto commanded the Japanese Navy in the early years of World War II. He was assigned the task of planning and leading the attack against Pearl Harbor and the air installations on Oahu. He disagreed with his country's decision to go to war against the United States, saying that the United States was too big a nation for Japan to defeat. The admiral was killed in 1943 in an air ambush in the South Pacific.

square miles of navigable waters. For almost a year, it had been serving as the home base for the U.S. Pacific Fleet.

Along with the people of Honolulu, the sailors at Pearl Harbor were enjoying the start of a quiet Sunday as Fuchida radioed his order to attack. In the next two hours, almost 2,400 Americans would die, and the harbor would be bathed in flames and covered with rolling clouds of oily smoke.

TWO:
DEATH AT
PEARL HARBOR

"To! To! To!" On receiving the order to attack, 91 of Mitsuo Fuchida's 183 planes banked away and flew toward Pearl Harbor. They consisted of fighters, torpedo bombers, high-altitude bombers, and dive bombers.

The Japanese plan called for the torpedo bombers to strike the harbor first. They were to be followed by the high-altitude bombers and then the dive bombers. The torpedo planes were to go in first because they moved more slowly than their companions. It was hoped that they would catch the enemy completely off guard. This would give them the chance to escape before the U.S. ships could begin defending themselves. Once the Americans opened fire, the slow-moving planes would become easy targets.

Within moments of leaving the formation, the Japanese pilots could see Pearl Harbor spread out before them. All around its edges were drydocks, workshops, supply depots, and oil storage tanks. At one far corner was a submarine base. Ships of all types—destroyers, cruisers, mine-sweepers, tenders, oil tankers, and harbor tugs—dotted the water. The only vessels not to be seen were the Pacific Fleet's three aircraft carriers—the *Enterprise,* the *Lexington,* and the *Saratoga.* They were on duty at sea.

The pilots of the first group headed for an island in the center of the harbor. This was Ford Island. It was blanketed with Navy offices and seaplane hangars. Along its east side lay the main target of the torpedo attack, the area known as Battleship Row. It was here that the battleships of the Pacific Fleet were moored.

Looking from north to south down Battleship Row, the Japanese pilots could see seven battleships anchored one after another in a neat line. From north to south, the ships were placed as follows: the *Nevada;* the *Arizona;* the *Tennessee* and, alongside it, the *West Virginia;* the *Maryland* and the *Oklahoma,* side by side; and the *California.* In addition, a repair ship, the *Vestal,* lay alongside the *Arizona.*

There was also a battleship moored on the opposite side of Ford Island—the *Utah.* An old vessel, it was no longer a fighting ship. Rather, the Navy used it as a target for gunnery practice at sea. Close by, a light cruiser, the *Raleigh,* rode at anchor.

The Japanese torpedo bombers, flying less than 50 feet above the water, swept into the harbor at 7:55 A.M. With each plane carrying a single torpedo, they came mostly in groups of three because the Japanese thought that it would take at least three of the slender missiles to sink a battleship. The first of the attacking groups released its deadly load, which hit the water and raced toward the *Raleigh* and the *Utah.* Three deafening explosions blew the *Utah* apart. The old fighter rolled over and went down.

The sinking of the *Utah* was a mistake. Since it was no longer a fighting vessel, the Japanese considered it a worthless target and a waste of torpedoes. But the commander of one torpedo group became confused at the last moment and attacked the ship.

Battleship Row under attack

A torpedo also slammed into the *Raleigh*. The cruiser staggered with the blow but did not sink. Its crew, though stunned by the unexpected attack, ran to their guns and succeeded in shooting down a dive bomber. It burst into flames, smashed into an aircraft tender, and set the ship afire.

BATTLESHIP ROW · Along Battleship Row itself, the torpedo planes swept in on their targets. One after the other, three torpedoes knifed into the *West Virginia*. Flames erupted from its decks. The ship sank into the mud.

Behind the *West Virginia* lay the *Oklahoma*. The first of three planes came at the ship. The pilot was just above the water when he released his torpedo. A second later, the *Oklahoma* shuddered as the torpedo struck home. Two more blasts followed as the other two pilots also scored direct hits.

The torpedoes damaged the *Oklahoma*'s electrical system and plunged the interior of the ship into darkness. Just minutes before, the crewmen had been relaxing in their bunks or eating breakfast. Now they struggled blindly to reach the outside deck. Most did not know what was happening and thought there had been some sort of accident on board.

When they came out into the sunlight, their ship was listing badly. Running along the tilting deck, they made their way to their battle stations. But the tilt steepened. Equipment tumbled across the deck. A desperate command was passed from man to man: "Abandon ship." Crewmen dove overboard or climbed down the ship's side and dropped into the water as the dying *Oklahoma* rolled completely over.

At one end of the line, the *California* shook with two torpedo blasts but stayed afloat. And at the other end of the line, the *Nevada* was hit. One of the *Nevada* sailors managed to reach a machine gun just as the planes shot past after releasing their missiles. His bullets sent one of the planes crashing into the harbor.

Three planes came at the *Arizona,* which was moored directly behind the *Nevada.* The pilots saw that the repair ship *Vestal* lay between them and their target. Their torpedoes passed beneath the *Vestal.* The *Arizona* heaved in agony as its bottom was torn away. But the worst was yet to come for the ship.

Flying high overhead, Mitsuo Fuchida watched the torpedo attack. He saw the Americans begin to open fire. He winced when some of his planes burst into flames and crashed. But he could not help but admire how quickly the surprised American sailors began to fight back.

The torpedo attack ended at a few minutes past 8:00 A.M. Now the high-altitude bombers, followed closely by the dive bombers, came roaring in over Pearl Harbor.

THE BOMBER ATTACK · At the start of the bomber attack, only two ships on Battleship Row had been lucky enough to escape harm. They were the *Maryland* and the *Tennessee.* Both had been protected from the torpedo planes by the ships that lay alongside them—the *West Virginia* and the *Oklahoma.* Safe from being hit, their gun crews had been able to send a withering fire against the attackers. One machine gunner, stationed high in the *Maryland*'s mast, riddled a torpedo plane with bullets. He saw it plunge earthward somewhere over Ford Island.

The luck of the two ships held as bombs now began to crash around them. There were explosions on all sides. But only two bombs found the *Maryland.* They did so little damage that the ship was quickly repaired in the next few days. Two bombs also struck the *Tennessee.* One killed several machine gunners. The other sliced through the roof of a gun turret. It did not explode. Instead, it shattered into pieces and began to burn.

Not so lucky was the *California.* The torpedo attack had left gaping holes below its waterline. The ship was slowly sinking. Now, as the bombers swept by overhead, a missile pierced its deck and exploded near the ship's sick bay, killing more than a hundred men. The *California* continued to sink. Its sailors went on firing their 5-inch batteries at the enemy planes.

The crew of the *Nevada,* hoping to save their torpedoed ship, tried to sail it out of the harbor. High-altitude and dive bombers went in pursuit as it limped into the channel that led to the open sea. There, several bombs found their mark. The ship's officers realized that the vessel was now so badly damaged that it would never reach the open sea. They ran the *Nevada* ashore on the east side of the channel.

A far worse fate befell the *Arizona.* With its bottom ripped away by a torpedo, the ship was now struck by eight bombs. Seconds later, a monstrous thunderclap rocked all of Pearl Harbor. Smoke and red flames shot more than 1,000 feet into the air as the *Arizona*'s powder magazine—its ammunition storeroom—exploded. The ship sank quickly and took 1,177 men to their deaths. They died in the blast or were drowned when they became trapped below decks.

The *U.S.S. California* slowly sinks as a result of bomb and torpedo damage.

DESTRUCTION EVERYWHERE · Even though it was the prime target, Battleship Row was not the only area under attack. Fuchida's bombers and fighters also struck at the drydocks,

piers, workshops, and supply depots that ringed the harbor. The assault on these facilities continued when the planes of the first wave finished their work and were replaced by those of the second wave.

The battleship *Pennsylvania* was in drydock and became a major target. Bombs fell all around it, damaging work cranes and tearing buildings apart, but the *Pennsylvania* suffered only one direct hit. Though thirteen of its men were killed and thirty-eight were injured in the blast, the ship itself sustained little damage.

But the same could not be said of another vessel in drydock, the destroyer *Shaw*. Struck by a bomb, it exploded in a blinding flash.

Other destroyers, cruisers, and work vessels were attacked as they lay at dockside or scrambled about the harbor in an effort to escape harm and fight back. Not only were they the targets of dive bombers, they were also strafed by the Japanese fighter planes. Their own guns added to the thunder of the morning.

ADM. HUSBAND E. KIMMEL
LT. GEN. WALTER C. SHORT

At the time of Pearl Harbor, Admiral Kimmel was in command of the U.S. Pacific Fleet, while General Short commanded the U.S. Army troops in Hawaii. Both men were severely criticized for not having their forces on greater alert against the possibility of a Japanese attack.

Whenever a ship sank, its crew took to small boats or dove into the water. Some of the men were picked up by nearby vessels. Some drowned. Some swam to shore through pools of burning oil from the surrounding wounded ships. Many were badly burned; others were completely naked, their clothing torn away by bomb blasts.

Everywhere they looked, they could see destruction. Buildings and hangars along the shore were being blown to pieces. Ships were afire out in the harbor. Thick black smoke poured into the sky from Battleship Row.

Slowly, however, the thunder of the guns and exploding bombs faded away. It was now 10 o'clock in the morning. The enemy planes disappeared over the horizon and returned to their carriers far out at sea. Still heard, however, were the cries of wounded men, the comforting words of those who went to help them, the shouts of those who fought the fires, and the roar of those fires. But, in comparison to the thunder of the past two hours, all seemed deathly quiet.

The attack on Pearl Harbor was over.

THREE:
DEATH ON
THE GROUND

"Our planes never had a chance to get off the ground." This was how many airmen described the fate of the air bases the Japanese had targeted for attack at the same time Pearl Harbor was being struck. Five bases came under fire: Wheeler Field, Bellows Field, Hickam Field, Ewa Field, and the Kaneohe Naval Air Station.

■ Both Wheeler Field and Bellows Field served as Army Air Corps fighter bases. There were also bombers stationed at Bellows.

Wheeler, located in the center of Oahu, was the larger of the two bases. The Japanese regarded it as a highly important target. Fuchida was under orders to hit it quickly and destroy its fighter planes before they could come to the aid of the ships in the harbor.

A group of his dive bombers and Zeros (fighter planes) carried out the attack. Engines screaming, they roared in over the field and streaked low above the rows of planes parked neatly alongside the runway. The planes were jolted as bombs exploded around them. Machine gun bullets riddled their fuselages and wings. Planes burst into flames when their gas-

Planes and hangars are wrecked during the Japanese attack on Wheeler Field.

oline tanks were ruptured. Pilots and ground crews tried to pull some of the undamaged ships away from those on fire but had to stop and take shelter when they themselves came under fire.

At the same time, bombs fell on the surrounding offices, workshops, and hangars. One bomb struck a barracks building. More than a hundred men inside were killed. Also hit by bombs and bullets was Schofield Barracks, an Army post next door to Wheeler.

Many of the attackers in Fuchida's wave—and in the second wave that followed—swooped so low that the people at Wheeler Field and Schofield Barracks could see the goggled faces of the pilots. Two dive bombers passed so close to some telephone lines that their wheels severed them. When the planes returned to their carrier, strips of the phone lines were found wrapped around their wheels.

At Bellows Field, located on the southeastern coast of Oahu, the first attack did little harm. A lone Japanese plane banked in from the ocean and strafed the base. Then came Fuchida's wave and the second wave. Buildings, hangars, and planes were set afire. As was true of all the bases, Bellows had few guns and was hard pressed to defend itself. But, as was also true of all the bases, the men there fought back as best they could, firing machine guns, rifles, and even pistols at the enemy.

Three U.S. aircraft—two observation planes and a B-17 bomber—attempted to take off. Zeros swarmed down on all three. One observation plane managed to get aloft, only to drop into the sea moments later. Both its companion ship and the B-17 were hit and crashed just as they were beginning to lift, skidding into the water at the end of the runway. The pilot who crashed at sea climbed out of his downed ship and swam ashore.

■ Situated on the east side of Pearl Harbor, Hickam Field served as an Army Air Corps bomber base. It, too, was hit by Fuchida's dive bombers and Zeros, and then by those of the second wave. All of them swept in just above ground level. The disasters at Wheeler and Bellows were repeated here. Parked aircraft burst into flames. Hangars were blown apart. The base gasoline dump exploded in an ugly cloud of smoke and flame.

Three B-17s from the United States were scheduled to land at Hickam that morning. They were due at dawn but were late in arriving because of a navigational error. As a result, they arrived in the middle of the attack.

All three were unarmed and helpless to defend themselves when a swarm of Zeros turned on them. The bomber pilots knew that they must land quickly if they were not to be shot out of the sky. For a moment, the pilots thought about fleeing to one of the nearby bases but then guessed that all the other fields would also be under attack. And so, with the Zeros chasing them, the three ships swept down onto the Hickam runway.

Two landed safely. The third, however, was set afire by enemy bullets. Its burning tail broke off as the plane touched down. The B-17 skidded wildly along the runway before finally coming to a stop with its nose pointing skyward.

■ Located just to the west of Pearl Harbor, Ewa was a Marine Corps field that housed both bombers and fighters. Kaneohe, a brand-new Navy facility, stood next to a small bay on Oahu's east coast. It was home base for thirty-six seaplanes.

Both bases suffered severe damage. Bombs and bullets set the aircraft at Ewa afire. The first seaplane to be hit at Kaneohe was moored in the bay. It burst into flames. Minutes later, its companions on shore were blazing, as were the station's hangars.

During the assault on Ewa, two U.S. fighters took off from a nearby small field that had been ignored by the Japanese. They swooped in among the attacking Zeros. The pilot of one fighter said that he was certain he had downed at least two enemy planes.

The two fighters were not the only U.S. planes to get into the air. They were joined by planes from the aircraft carrier *Enterprise,* which was just returning home from sea duty and was now some miles offshore. It is known that they downed at least three Japanese planes. There may have been more.

In a brief lull between the departure of Fuchida's wave and the arrival of the second wave, the sailors at Kaneohe rushed to their burning seaplanes. They pushed one down a ramp and into the water to extinguish the flames. Then they threw ropes around the blazing wing of another and attached the ropes to a tractor. The tractor pulled the wing free and saved the rest of the plane from being destroyed.

QUIET RETURNS · As was the case at Pearl Harbor, the attack on the air bases ended at about 10 o'clock. The Japanese planes headed back to their carriers, leaving behind one scene of devastation after another.

At Pearl Harbor, three battleships—the *Oklahoma,* the *Arizona,* and the *West Virginia*—were lost to the Navy for

Navy aircraft is set afire at Ewa Field.

good. The *Nevada* was aground. The *California* was sinking. The *Maryland,* the *Tennessee,* and the *Pennsylvania* were damaged, but they could be repaired. Eleven other warships—destroyers and cruisers—were sunk or badly damaged.

The air bases reported that 188 planes had been reduced to heaps of burning wreckage. Another 159 were damaged. Wheeler Field counted more than 60 planes destroyed. The losses at Hickam added up to more than 50 aircraft. At Ewa, the total stood at 30. Kaneohe lost 27 of its flying boats.

Most tragic of all was the loss of life. Dead were 2,330 American servicemen. The toll rose to just under 2,400 when 69 civilians were reported killed. Almost half the dead—1,177—were the men who died when the *Arizona*'s magazine exploded.

But the Japanese did not escape without harm. Once the first moments of surprise and confusion were past, the Navy guns were joined by some nearby Army batteries. Their combined fire downed 29 planes and took the lives of 64 Japanese fliers.

Also lost were six enemy midget submarines. These were operating just off the coast of Oahu. Their role in the attack was to sneak into Pearl Harbor and add to the havoc. They were sighted and destroyed by U.S. warships on patrol just offshore.

Actually, the first vessel lost at Pearl Harbor was a Japanese submarine. Sighted by a patrolling destroyer just outside the harbor entrance, it was sunk with gunfire and depth charges. The commander of another wounded sub ran his craft aground. He became the first enemy to be taken prisoner by the United States in World War II.

FOUR:
THE ROAD TO
PEARL HARBOR

Word of the attack on Pearl Harbor reached the United States that Sunday about 1:30 P.M., Eastern Standard Time. It sent a shock wave throughout the entire country.

Some Americans, though surprised by its suddenness, were not really surprised by the attack. They knew that Japan had long aimed at becoming the dominant power in East Asia and the western reaches of the Pacific Ocean. In seeking that goal, Japan had been traveling a road that was certain to lead to war with the United States.

Japan's quest for domination began in 1931 when its troops invaded and won control of Manchuria in northern China. Next, in 1937, Japan went to war against China. The Japanese leaders thought that only a few months would be needed to subdue that country, but the Chinese stubbornly held off the invaders for the rest of the decade.

The fighting put a terrible drain on Japan's military capacity. The nation had scant natural resources of its own. It had to depend on other countries for the goods needed to fuel its war machine. Most of those goods came from the United States. Even though Washington was angered by the Japanese attack on China, American manufacturers continued

New York World-Telegram

SCRIPPS-HOWARD

Local Forecast: Light rains tonight, somewhat higher temperatures than last night; tomorrow cloudy followed by clearing, cooler than today.

Copyright, 1941, by New York World-Telegram Corporation. All rights reserved.

VOL. 74.—NO. 135.—IN TWO SECTIONS—SECTION ONE   NEW YORK, MONDAY, DECEMBER 8, 1941.   Entered as second class matter Post Office, New York, N. Y.

LATEST WALL ST. PRICES
Real Estate, Page 31
PRICE THREE CENTS

1500 DEAD IN HAWAII
CONGRESS VOTES WAR

Tally in Senate Is 82 to 0, In House 388 to 1, with Miss Rankin Sole Objector

By LYLE C. WILSON.
United Press Staff Correspondent.

WASHINGTON, Dec. 8.—Congress today proclaimed existence of a state of war between the United States and the Japanese Empire 33 minutes after President Roosevelt stood before a joint session to ask such action and pledge that we will triumph—"so help us, God."

Democracy was proving its right to a place in the sun with a split-second shiftover from peace to all-out war.

The Senate acted first, adopting the resolution by a unanimous roll call vote of 82 to 0, within 21 minutes after the President had concluded his address, amid tumultuous cheering of both houses.

The House vote was 388 to 1.

The lone dissenting vote was cast by Representative Rankin (R., Mont.). It was she who in the small hours of April 6, 1917, faltered, wept and finally voted no against a similar resolution aimed at Germany. A chorus of hisses and boos greeted her vote.

Representative Knutson (R., Minn.), who also voted against American entry into the World War in 1917, said today this nation "has no choice but to declare war on Japan."

"I do not see that we have any other choice," Mr. Knutson told reporters. "They declared war on us."

Miss Rankin and Mr. Knutson sae the only present members of the House who voted against war in 1917.

Only Miss Rankin and Representative Hoffman (R. Mich.) had remained seated when the House gave a standing ovation in response to President Roosevelt's solemn statement.

"I ask that the Congress declare that since the unprovoked and dastardly attack by Japan on Sunday, Dec. 7, a state of war has existed between the United States and the Japanese empire."

All Measures for Defense.

In a staccato of short sentences, the President told where the Japanese had hit yesterday throughout the Pacific area and how their representatives "here had at the same time been continuing deceptive and false negotiations for maintenance of peace. And, be

(Continued on Page Eleven.)

The Weather

(Official United States Forecast.)
New York and Metropolitan area—Light rains tonight and rains tonight; somewhat higher temperature than last night; tomorrow cloudy followed by clearing, cooler than today; strong winds becoming strong; tomorrow cloudy followed by clearing, cooler than today; occasional winds highest temperature expected tomorrow, 46.

New Jersey—Cloudy and somewhat warmer, occasional light rains tonight; tomorrow mostly cloudy followed by somewhat colder.

Connecticut—Snow, changing to occasional light rain, warmer tonight; tomorrow clearing, not much colder in late afternoon or night.

New York temperature expected tonight: 50.
Lowest temperature last night: 38.

Roosevelt's War Message To Congress

By the United Press.
WASHINGTON, Dec. 8.—The text of President Roosevelt's war message to Congress:

TO THE CONGRESS OF THE UNITED STATES:
Yesterday, Dec. 7, 1941—a date which will live in infamy—the United States of America was suddenly and deliberately attacked by naval and air forces of the Empire of Japan.

The United States was at peace with that nation and, at the solicitation of Japan, was still in conversation with its government and its Emperor, looking toward the maintenance of peace in the Pacific.

Indeed, one hour after Japanese air squadrons had commenced bombing in Oahu, the Japanese Ambassador to the United States and his colleague delivered to the Secretary of State a formal reply to a recent American message. While this reply stated that it seemed useless to continue the existing diplomatic negotiations, it

(Continued on Page Twelve.)

All Draft Quotas To Be Increased

By the United Press.
BOISE, Idaho, Dec. 8.—Se-

Britain Declares War on Japan

Becomes Ally of U. S., China and Thailand

By the Associated Press.
LONDON, Dec. 8.—Britain, like the United States under Japanese attack, declared war today on the Japanese government without waiting for Washington first to formalize its American declaration.

Said Prime Minister Churchill: "It only remains now for the great democracies to face their tasks with whatever strength God may give them."

At the same time Britain made allies of Thailand and Free China. Prime Minister Churchill told a joint session of the British Empire that Japan attacked it at 1 p. m. E S T in a 250-word note through the preliminary tea time. If It takes three till said—

Axis and U. S. at War, Rome Radio Asserts

The Rome Radio told today that Germany considered the United States at war with the Axis because

Navy Enlistment Office Swamped by Volunteers

Number Quitting Jobs to Join Is Double That of Last War

All over town today young men—and quite a few old ones with wives and children—were going up to the boss and saying "I quit!" By the hundreds, from the Bronx to Staten Island, they overran the Army, Navy and Marine recruiting offices with such gusto that the Navy had to close down for the day shortly after noon.

In response to what naval authorities said was a "critical" load of men fully 1000 showed up to volunteer, besides another 500 seeking Marine berths and about another 300 Army recruits. The navy said not only that its offices were swamped this day but also that the boss let his world closed door yesterday at 1 p. m.

night, but they had to shut the door till the face of all late comers.

The navy volunteering ran more than twice as high as for the first day of war in 1917, and the possible need of a naval draft, which believed the 15 per cent recruit-

ing lag after the Reuben James disaster, became remote. Hereafter all the recruiting offices will be on a seven-day, 24-hour basis while the Coast Guard recruiting office, 1 State St., goes on an 1 a. m.-3 p. m. schedule, except for Sundays.

All night long recruits besieged the Navy Recruiting Office at 90 Church St., and by the time its offices were opened, there was a line of about 800 men, three abreast reaching all the way down Barclay St. to West Broadway. At 35 Whitehall St., where the Army Building is located, there was a night-long procession, too, though on a considerably smaller scale. There was much laughing and

(Continued on Page Twelve.)

U. S., Japanese Fleets Believed in Battle

By the United Press.
HONOLULU, Dec. 8.—United States and Japanese fleets were believed fighting in mid-Pacific today after a naval engagement off the Hawaiian Islands.

Japan Claims Naval Supremacy

Four Battleships Reported Hit

(Continued on Page Twelve.)

100 to 200 Soldiers Killed in Japanese Raid On Luzon in Philippines

BULLETIN.
By the United Press.
MANILA, Dec. 8.—Press dispatches reported that 100 to 200 troops, 60 of them Americans, were killed or injured today when Japanese warplanes raided Iba, on the west coast of the island of Luzon, north of the Olangapo naval base.

BULLETIN.
Radio messages heard in New York at 2:10 p. m. this afternoon indicated that an air raid then was in progress over Manila.

NBC's correspondent reported at 2:30 p. m. that Manila has just been bombed.

By the United Press.
WASHINGTON, Dec. 8. — Casualties on the Hawaiian island of Oahu in yesterday's Japanese air attack will amount to about 3000, including about 1500 fatalities, the White House announced today.

The White House confirmed the loss in Pearl Harbor of "one old battleship" and a destroyer, which was blown up.

Several other American ships were damaged and a large number of army and navy airplanes on Hawaiian fields were put out of commission, the White House disclosed.

It reported at the same time that American operations against Japan were being carried out on a large scale, resulting already in the destruction of "a number of Japanese planes and submarines."

The White House statement said:

"American operations against the Japanese attacking force in the neighborhood of the Hawaiian Islands are still continuing. A number of Japanese planes and submarines have been destroyed.

"The damage caused to our forces in Oahu in yesterday's attack appears more serious' than at first believed.

"In Pearl Harbor itself one old battleship has capsized and several other ships have been seriously damaged.

"One destroyer was blown up. Several other small ships were seriously hurt. Army and navy fields were bombed with the resulting destruction of several hangars. A large number of planes were put out of commission.

"A number of bombers arrived safely from San Francisco during the engagement—while it was under way. Reinforcements of planes are being rushed and repair work is under way on the ships, planes and ground facilities.

"Guam, Wake and Midway Islands and Hong Kong have been attacked. Details of these attacks are lacking.

"Two hundred marines—all that remain in China—have been interned by the Japanese near Tientsin.

"The total number of casualties on the island of Oahu are not yet definitely known but, in all probability, will mount to about 3000. Nearly half of these

Over this vast stage the newest showdown war is being fought out today. In the Philippines (1) Japanese bombers struck twice during the day at Davao, Baguio and Fort Stotsenburg, with Japan also claiming American planes downed at Clark Field and the Japanese troops advanced on Hongkong (2), and battled the British on the beaches of Malaya (3), where Japanese planes hit Singapore. Thailand (4) appeared ready to yield passage to Japanese invading from the sea and Indo-China. The American Pacific fleet prepared to battle from Pearl Harbor, in Hawaii (5), after Japanese raids aimed at battleships and killed men in Hickam Field barracks. Elsewhere the far-flung Japanese forces occupied Shanghai, seizing an American communications ship and sinking a British gunboat; laid siege to Guam, reportedly captured Wake Island (6), and raided Nauru (7).

■ U.S. BASES
■ JAPANESE BASES

World-Telegram Map.

to sell the Japanese oil, gasoline, iron, and scrap steel during the 1930s.

In 1939, when Adolf Hitler set out to conquer the nations around him and plunged Europe into war, the United States stayed out of the fighting. It did so in great part because many of its people could not forget the hurt the country had suffered during the First World War. Vast numbers of Americans and many of the nation's leaders wanted no part of another foreign war. They said that foreign wars were none of America's business.

But President Franklin D. Roosevelt—along with most Americans—viewed Germany's Hitler as a hateful dictator and began to help the nations opposing him. In March 1941 the Lend-Lease Act was passed by Congress, giving Roosevelt the authority to send aid to any country he felt needed it. Food and military supplies were sent to a number of Hitler's enemies, chief among them Great Britain.

FRANKLIN D. ROOSEVELT

Elected to the office in 1932, 1936, 1940, and 1944, Franklin D. Roosevelt served as president of the United States during World War II until his death in April 1945, just a few weeks before the fighting in Europe ended and a few months before Japan surrendered.

Thus, while remaining neutral, the United States did not look on Germany and its partner, Italy, as friends. Japan was also seen as a potential enemy. This was because of a treaty that Germany and Japan had signed in 1936, declaring that they would assist each other in the event of war. Germany, Italy, and Japan became known as the Axis Powers.

In 1940, Hitler attacked and quickly defeated France. This victory triggered a new action by Japan. Its troops entered the French colony in Southeast Asia known then as Indochina. (Today, Indochina is divided into three independent nations: Vietnam, Laos, and Cambodia, or Kampuchea.)

The Indochina situation worried President Roosevelt and other American leaders. They suspected that the Japanese planned to use Indochina as the springboard for an assault on two nearby areas: Malaya and the islands of the East Indies (today called Indonesia). Malaya was a British possession, while the East Indies were held by the Dutch. Japan's aim would be to gain control of these countries' rich natural resources—especially oil and metals—for its war machine.

President Roosevelt decided to act against the aggressive nation. He prohibited all trade with Japan and cut off the flow of desperately needed U.S. oil, gasoline, and metals.

It was a move that put a new and terrible drain on Japan's resources. The United States then told Japan that it would reopen trade only if all Japanese troops were removed from Indochina. This left Japan with just two choices. It could either suffer the humiliation of giving in to the American demand or attack Malaya and the Dutch East Indies and grab the resources there.

THE JAPANESE CHOICE · Japan chose the latter course and elected to attack a string of American and British targets in the Pacific. Its aim, of course, was to cripple the American and British forces so that they would be helpless to stop the grab for Malayan and East Indian natural resources. In addition, Japan knew that many Americans wanted no part of foreign wars. The Japanese leadership hoped that Washington would also want to avoid going to war in the Pacific and would step aside and let Japan do what it wished there.

The Japanese selected as their targets not only the Hawaiian islands but also several American possessions in the Pacific, including the Philippines, Guam, Wake Island, and Midway Island; two British possessions, including Hong Kong and Malaya; and the independent nation of Siam.

Even while planning the attack, Japan sent a representative to Washington to discuss the reopening of trade with the United States. On December 7, he and the Japanese ambassador to America were seated in the office of the secretary of state with a message from their government concerning the trade talks when word of the Pearl Harbor attack came through.

CORDELL HULL

Cordell Hull was the U.S. secretary of state from 1933 to 1944. Kichisaburo Nomura, the Japanese ambassador to the United States, and Saburo Kurusu, the representative sent by the Japanese government in late 1941 for talks about reopening U.S. trade, were seated in Secretary Hull's office when news of the Pearl Harbor disaster reached America.

MIDWAY
ISLANDS

Wake Island

P A C I F I C

MARIANA
ISLANDS
Guam

O C E A N

MARSHALL
ISLANDS

CAROLINE ISLANDS

Equator

NEW
GUINEA

Actually, despite the talks, the United States knew that the Japanese had chosen to attack rather than obey the American demand to leave Indochina. The choice was known because the Americans had broken the secret code that Japan used to pass messages to its foreign embassies. But one crucial fact remained a mystery—the location of the attack. Because Japanese ship movements had been detected in the South Pacific, many of President Roosevelt's military advisers mistakenly guessed that the primary assault would come in oil-rich Malaya.

On Monday, December 8, 1941, President Roosevelt appeared before a joint session of Congress to deliver one of the most memorable speeches in the nation's history. He began with the words:

> *Yesterday, December 7, 1941—a date which will live in infamy—the United States of America was suddenly and deliberately attacked by naval and air forces of the Empire of Japan.*

The president went on to say that, at the time of the attack, America had been at peace with Japan and that the two nations had been talking about reopening their trade. Then he said:

> *It will be recorded that the distance of Hawaii from Japan makes it obvious that the attack was deliberately planned many days or even weeks ago. During the intervening time the Japanese Government has deliberately sought to deceive the United States by false statements and expressions of hope for continued peace.*

President Roosevelt asks Congress for a declaration of war against Japan.

He next turned to the actions that had gone hand-in-hand with the assault on Pearl Harbor:

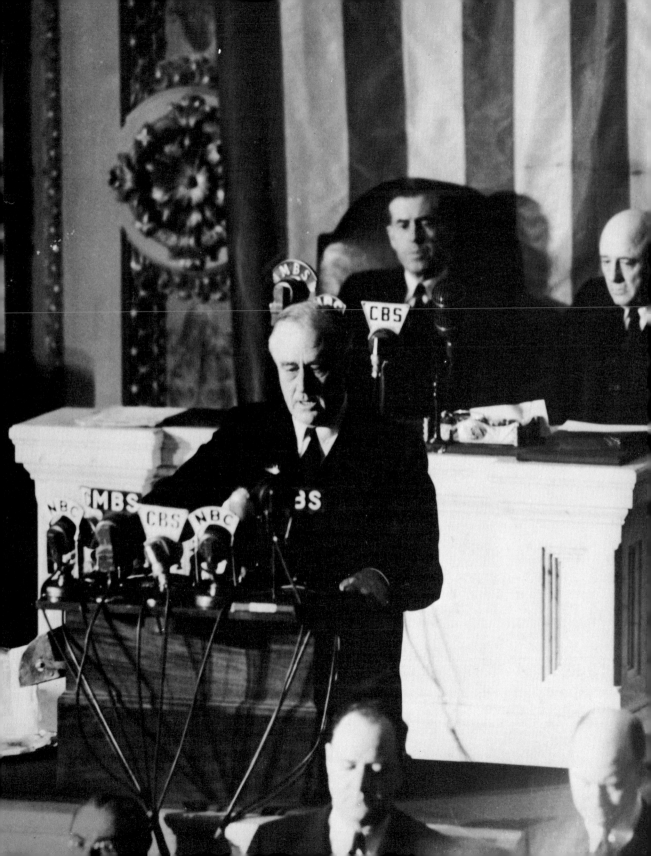

Yesterday the Japanese Government also launched an attack against Malaya . . . Last night Japanese forces attacked Hong Kong . . . Guam . . . the Philippine islands . . . Wake Island . . . And this morning the Japanese attacked Midway Island. Japan has therefore undertaken a surprise offensive extending throughout the Pacific area . . .

The president said that he had "directed that all measures be taken" for the nation's defense. Then:

No matter how long it may take us to overcome this premeditated invasion, the American people, in their righteous might, will win through to absolute victory . . . we will not only defend ourselves to the uttermost but will make it very certain that this form of treachery will never again endanger us . . . I ask that the Congress declare that since the unprovoked and dastardly attack by Japan on Sunday, December 7, 1941, a state of war has existed between the United States and the Japanese Empire.

Congress quickly granted Roosevelt's request and declared war on Japan. Three days later, on December 11, Japan's fellow Axis Powers—Germany and Italy—declared war on the United States. The United States replied with a return declaration of war. Great Britain joined the United States in the war against Japan.

Until these many declarations, the world had been enduring two separate conflicts, the Japanese-Chinese war in Asia and the war in Europe. But now these wars had become entwined and become one—World War II.

FIVE: LIGHTNING ATTACKS

The attacks that were launched the same day that Pearl Harbor was being assaulted all shared one thing in common. They were complete successes for the Japanese.

As you now read about them, you may be puzzled to see that most are listed as occurring on Monday, December 8, rather than Sunday, December 7, 1941. The reason for the difference is that all but two of the targets lay to the west of the International Date Line, which runs down through the Pacific Ocean. The day was Sunday for the Hawaiian islands and Midway, which are east of the line. But it was Monday west of the line.

SOUTHEAST ASIA · The Japanese move against Malaya on December 8 began on the northeast coast of the peninsula. The first of what would grow to more than 200,000 Japanese troops poured ashore. Arriving aboard ships that had brought them from nearby Indochina, they immediately began to move southward. Their goal was the southern tip of the peninsula, some 350 miles away. It was the island of Singapore, the home of a giant British military stronghold.

British troops sped north to repel the invasion. But, heavily outnumbered, they could not stop the Japanese advance. The next seventy days saw the invaders battle their way through swamps and jungles to Singapore. The island and its great fortress surrendered on February 15, 1942. Some 65,000 British soldiers and sailors were taken prisoner. All of Malaya was in enemy hands.

As the first landings were taking place at Malaya, Japanese troops in Indochina were also on the move. They plunged across the border and into neighboring Siam. The Siamese, overwhelmed by the enemy's strength, were able to fight back for no more than five hours. By the afternoon of December 9, Siam's capital city, Bangkok, fell to the invaders. With its fall, the Japanese gained control of the entire Malay Peninsula.

Soon after claiming Siam, the Japanese took two additional steps. First, in mid-December, they invaded the island of Borneo to the southeast of Indochina. Then, using Borneo as a springboard, they moved south against the target that ranked with Malaya as a treasure house of natural resources, the Dutch East Indies. They crushed a small fleet of American, Australian, and Dutch warships that tried to block their way. By March 1942, Japan held the East Indies in its grip.

Also, late in December 1941, Japanese troops overran Burma, a British possession that bordered Siam on the west. They had most of Burma under their thumb by the spring of 1942.

HONG KONG · There were 11,000 British and Canadian troops stationed in Hong Kong when it was bombed from the air and shelled from the sea on December 8. The bombers destroyed all but one of the eight aircraft parked on the island's airfield.

The enemy landed and cut off the supply of water to the defending forces. The British and Canadian troops gave up the fight on Christmas Day.

The December 8 attack on Hong Kong was accompanied by two assaults on the coast of China itself, where Japanese troops captured the American Army and Navy garrisons in Shanghai and Tientsen.

MIDWAY, GUAM, AND WAKE ISLAND were all bombed or shelled within hours of the attack on Pearl Harbor. Midway, about 1,300 miles northwest of Hawaii, housed a Navy air and submarine base. It escaped the fate that befell both Guam and Wake Island. Though pounded hard by enemy planes and ships, Midway was not invaded. It was not considered important enough for capture.

Following a series of air bombings, 6,000 Japanese troops landed at Guam on December 11. They waded ashore on an island that was without artillery of any sort. Guam had never been fortified. The island stood close to Japan, with just 1,100 miles separating the two. Washington had feared that, if steps were taken to arm the place, the Japanese would be provoked into an attack.

There were 430 U.S. troops on Guam when the invasion force appeared. The Americans had no choice but to surrender.

The story at Wake Island was quite different. Five hours after the attack on Pearl Harbor, a fleet of thirty-six bombers came roaring through a heavy rain from the Japanese-held atoll of Kwajalein 600 miles away. They unloaded their deadly

cargoes on the island's airfield while Zeros strafed the runways and hangars. Thirty-four Americans were killed or wounded in the attack.

Wake Island, 1,800 miles west of Hawaii, was manned by 400 U.S. Marines. With them were 1,100 civilian construction workers. In the 1930s, the island had served as a landing spot for commercial Pan American airplanes. Only recently had it been turned into a military base. The construction workers were putting the finishing touches on a new runway and were starting to erect hangars when the Japanese struck.

The bombing of December 8 was followed by others in the next days. Then, just before dawn on December 11, the Marines and construction workers sighted a fleet of thirteen Japanese ships bearing down on them. The Marines manned their only artillery pieces—a string of old 5-inch guns that had been placed on the island after years of battleship service.

Patiently, the Marines stood by their batteries and waited for the invasion fleet to sail within range. Only then did they open fire. The light cruiser at the head of the Japanese force was hit twice. It turned and fled, with its fellow ships steaming close behind. Because of the bombings, there were only four American fighter-bombers left on the island. They set off after the retreating enemy. On their return, the pilots reported that they had seen the wounded cruiser sink. They themselves had sent a destroyer to the bottom and had damaged seven other vessels. It was later learned that some 500 enemy soldiers and sailors had died during the failed invasion. Just four Marines had been wounded.

One artist's rendering of the invasion of Guam.

Though jubilant over their victory, the Marines knew that another invasion attempt was sure to come. For the next two weeks, they worked round the clock to improve their defenses and repair the bomb damage. Laboring alongside them in the tropical sun and heavy rains were 300 construction workers. All the other workers had fled to various parts of the island for safety. All the while, enemy bombers and fighters attacked the island. Their bombs and bullets chewed up the runway, destroyed the remaining four fighter-bombers, blew hangars to pieces, and tore the defenses apart.

As the men worked, they wondered when the next invasion attempt would come—and when, if ever, the United States would send reinforcements to assist them. Actually, a small fleet, led by the aircraft carrier *Saratoga,* was on its way from Pearl Harbor. But it failed to reach the island in time to be of help. Just after 2 o'clock on the morning of a moonless December 23, the expected invasion became a reality.

MAJ. JAMES P. S. DEVEREUX

Major Devereux commanded the U.S. Marines and construction workers who staged the courageous defense of Wake Island.

It was so dark that the Marine lookouts did not see the attackers until moments before a thousand troops stormed ashore. Instantly, machine gun fire began to rake the dark figures plunging through the surf and onto the beach. One of the 5-inchers managed to set an enemy ship afire. But this time there was no stopping the invaders as they charged the gun positions. The battle turned into brutal hand-to-hand fighting as the Japanese overran each position. Slowly, the exhausted defenders fell back toward the center of the island.

The battle ended a few minutes past 7 A.M. that December 23. Completely encircled by the enemy, the Marines and construction workers surrendered. But the fight for Wake had cost the invaders dearly, with some 700 men lost in comparison with 122 defenders dead. Of the 122 dead Americans, 52 were Marines and sailors. Seventy were construction workers.

In the weeks after Pearl Harbor, the American people were not only angered and stunned but also humiliated by the seemingly endless string of Japanese victories. The magnificent defense of Wake Island helped them to quickly rebuild their pride in the American fighting forces. They would feel the same way about the defense of the Philippine islands.

SIX:
THE ATTACK ON
THE PHILIPPINES

In 1941, the Philippine islands were the largest of America's holdings in the Pacific. From the late 1500s to the end of the nineteenth century, they had been a possession of Spain but had passed into U.S. hands after the Spanish-American War of 1898. They consisted of more than 7,000 islands that ranged in size from small, uninhabited bits of land to one—Luzon—that was about as large as the state of Ohio.

Long before coming under American rule, the Filipino people had campaigned to have their homeland become an independent nation. In 1934, the United States agreed to grant the islands complete independence at the end of a twelve-year period, in 1946. In preparation for the freedom that would then be theirs, the Philippine people had drawn up their own constitution, established a legislative body, and named a president.

Luzon, which was not only the largest of the island group but also the home of the Philippine government, was the first to suffer at enemy hands. At a little after noontime on December 8, fifty-four bombers roared in overhead. They came from bases on Formosa, a Japanese-held island about 700 miles to the north. Their targets were two air bases—Clark Field and Iba Field. Both were located near the nation's capital city, Manila.

Within minutes, the same fate suffered by the airfields around Pearl Harbor was repeated. Destroyed on the ground at Clark and Iba were at least 56 fighters, 18 B-17s, and 25 other planes. The lost planes added up to more than half of the U.S. aircraft in the Philippines.

On December 9, another flight of enemy bombers arrived from Formosa and swept over the Cavite naval base, which was located on Manila Bay near the city of Manila. Bombs rained down on the ships of the U.S. Asiatic Fleet, a force made up chiefly of cruisers and destroyers. Fortunately, most of the ships escaped serious damage. Many were away from the base and sailing in the South Pacific. Those that had remained at home now dashed out of Manila Bay to the safety of the sea.

Then, just before Christmas, the Philippine islands were struck by two invasions. On December 20, enemy troops came ashore and took the island of Mindanao far to the south of Luzon. The next day, the 100,000-man Japanese 14th Army began a move against Luzon itself. The invaders surged on to the beaches at Lingayen Gulf, a band of water that cut its way into the western coast of Luzon some 110 miles north of Manila. Their orders were to take the capital city and bring all of Luzon to its knees in the next fifty days.

Painting of the Cavite naval base under attack.

GENERAL DOUGLAS MACARTHUR · The job of defending the Philippines against the invaders was in the hands of General Douglas MacArthur. Under his command were three forces—

the Philippine Army of 100,000 men, an American infantry division of 20,000 men, and a contingent of 10,000 men known as the Philippine Scouts. The Scouts were rugged Filipino fighters who served as part of the U.S. Army.

In 1937, when he was fifty-six years old, MacArthur had retired from the U.S. Army so that he could accept a post that had been offered to him by the president of the Philippines, Manuel Quezon. President Quezon was an old friend who had known MacArthur when the general had commanded the U.S. forces in the Philippines in the 1920s. He wanted MacArthur to build a Filipino army so that it would be in place for the defense of the nation when independence came in 1946.

On accepting the post, MacArthur had been named to the rank of Field Marshal by Quezon. American troops had been placed under his command to help train the new army. Then, in 1941, when the threat of war loomed large after the United States cut off its trade with Japan, MacArthur had been called

GEN. DOUGLAS MACARTHUR

In early 1942, during the last-ditch defense of the Philippine islands, President Roosevelt ordered General MacArthur to leave Corregidor and travel to Australia. The General was then appointed the Allied supreme commander of the Southwest Pacific area.

back into the U.S. Army. He had been given command of all the troops in the Philippine islands, American and Filipino alike.

CLOSING IN FROM TWO SIDES · MacArthur's Filipino army was not yet fully trained for battle when the Japanese stormed ashore at Lingayen Gulf. Further, there were hardly any planes left to give his men support from the air. And so one terrible report after another flowed into his headquarters at Manila. The Filipino and American soldiers who had met the invasion were being mercilessly driven back toward the capital city. It was only a matter of time before the enemy entered Manila.

A particularly disturbing report arrived two days before Christmas. A new Japanese force was invading Luzon. It had landed at Lamon Bay some 60 miles to MacArthur's south. The enemy was now closing in on him from two sides. He knew that Manila would fall any day now.

CAPT. COLIN P. KELLY

Captain Kelly was the pilot of one of the planes that escaped harm in the first bombings of the Philippines. A few days later, he flew his B-17 bomber against a Japanese fleet that was sighted near Luzon. Three of his bombs struck and severely damaged the battleship *Haruna*. Before he could escape, his plane was shot down and he died in the crash. Along with the men who were defending Pearl Harbor, Captain Kelly became one of the first American heroes of the war.

Faced with certain defeat, MacArthur ordered all his troops to withdraw to Bataan, a peninsula of rock and jungle on the northern side of the entrance to Manila Bay. They were ordered to take up positions there for a last-ditch stand.

On Christmas Eve, with the enemy drawing nearer and nearer, MacArthur and his staff climbed aboard a small steamboat and rode out to a small island near the entrance to Manila Bay. There, he set up headquarters in the tunnels of a heavily defended military post. The island was Corregidor. Everyone called it by its nickname, ''The Rock.''

Vicious fighting marked every step of the way in the move to Bataan. Both MacArthur's troops and the enemy suffered heavy losses. The Japanese nipped at the heels of the retreating soldiers, attacking time and again. The Filipinos and Americans fought off the attacks and retaliated with some of their own. Finally, toward the end of December, they arrived at Bataan and began to dig defensive positions for themselves.

There, at Bataan and on Corregidor, the Americans and Filipinos were to stage the final defense of the Philippine Islands. Short of food, exhausted, and stricken with tropical diseases, they would fight on for four months before being overwhelmed in April 1942. The story of their courageous fight and the cruelties they had to endure after surrendering will be told in the next book in this series.

SEVEN: THE AMERICAN PEOPLE AT WAR

The emotions of the American people ran high in the weeks that followed December 7, 1941. First, there was deep shock at the damage inflicted by the Japanese at Pearl Harbor. In a single day, life in the United States had completely changed.

Then there was anger that the assault had come without warning. Americans everywhere branded it a loathsome "sneak" attack. Adding to their anger was the fact that a Japanese representative had been in Washington that very Sunday to talk about reopening trade between the two countries. Many Americans saw this as the most underhanded act of all. To them, it meant that "The Japanese were kidding us by talking one way and acting the other way."

And there was a deep fear along the West Coast. People in California, Oregon, and Washington State expected the Japanese to follow Pearl Harbor with an invasion of the Hawaiian islands and then an invasion of the Pacific coast states. Neither invasion ever came to pass. The plan for the Pearl Harbor attack had not included such invasions. The attack's sole aim had been to cripple the U.S. naval and air forces there.

There was also the fear that the Pacific coast would be bombed from the air or shelled from the sea. This fear became a reality in early 1942 when a Japanese submarine fired on an oil refinery in Santa Barbara, California. Only slight harm was done. Some weeks later, an enemy submarine shelled the Oregon coast. Again, the harm was slight. Then a Japanese plane flew in from a carrier and dropped a number of bombs on an Oregon forest, setting a few small fires.

ILL PREPARED FOR WAR · In addition to their other emotions, many Americans were angry with their own government. They felt that the United States had acted unwisely during the 1930s. It had, they charged, failed to prepare the nation for war at a time when everyone knew that Japan and Hitler's Germany were planning to take over great chunks of the world.

These Americans said there were two reasons why their country should have prepared itself for war. First, if the nations of Europe could not defend themselves against Hitler's planned conquests, the United States would have the responsibility of trying to save them. Second, if Germany and Japan ever won all that they wanted, there would be nothing to stop them from attacking the United States.

But there were also two reasons why the United States did not spend the entire 1930s girding itself for war. First, as was said earlier, vast numbers of Americans and many of the nation's leaders wanted no part of any new foreign conflicts because of the suffering the country had endured in World War I. Next, the United States was caught in the Great Depression. Its people could not afford to provide the money needed to prepare for war.

A few days after Pearl Harbor, the San Francisco phone company hastily put up this barrier of sandbags against Japanese bombs that never came.

As a result, the early 1930s saw the government devote little money to military spending. They also saw a great debate rage throughout the nation. On one side were the Americans who wanted to avoid war at all costs. On the other were those who argued that the country must ready itself to fight two aggressor nations.

However, though poorly prepared at the time of Pearl Harbor, the United States was not completely unprepared for trouble. President Roosevelt had long seen that Hitler and Japan were leading the world toward global conflict. He began to strengthen America's defenses in the late 1930s.

In 1938 and 1939, the president was successful in persuading Congress to increase the nation's spending for defense. Then, in 1940, Congress took two major steps at Roosevelt's urging. A military budget was passed that started the United States on the way to a 200-ship Navy. Next, Congress enacted the Selective Training and Service Act. This act enabled the country to begin drafting men into the armed forces.

The act called for men between the ages of 21 and 35 to serve a year in uniform, after which they would be released. Then, should war come, they would already be trained as soldiers. In 1941, the length of service was stretched to eighteen months. Finally, after the attack on Pearl Harbor, it was extended to six months after the end of the war.

The unemployed line up for bread and coffee at St. Peter's Mission in New York City during the Great Depression.

Also changed were the age ranges for the draft. In 1940, they were extended to the ages of 20 to 44. The lower end of the range was later dropped to 18. As it turned out, the government did not find it necessary to draft any man over age 38.

Men had been drafted during the Civil War and World War I, but the 1940 act gave the United States its first peacetime draft. By the time of Pearl Harbor, 1.6 million American men and women were in uniform.

Preparations for war could also be seen in the December talks about reopening trade with Japan. You'll recall that the United States had broken Japan's secret code and knew that an attack was being planned. Nevertheless, the United States agreed to talks with the Japanese representative. This was done to "buy time"—to give the country a few extra days to send military supplies to its Pacific bases.

A COUNTRY UNITED · As soon as the Japanese struck at Pearl Harbor, the American people quickly drew together in the defense of their country. Forgotten was the split of the 1930s over whether the United States should become involved in any foreign war. Men and women everywhere hurried to enlist in the armed forces. By the time the war ended, a total of 16 million men and women had seen service in the armed forces of the United States.

Millions of other American men and women went to work in defense factories as the nation's industries got down to the work of producing war materials. Between January 1, 1942, and the end of the fighting in 1945, the country's industrial might produced a staggering amount of war materials. Among them were some 315,000 artillery pieces, 86,000 tanks, 64,500 landing craft, 6,500 fighting ships, and 5,400 cargo vessels.

Once they drew together in the defense of their country, the people of the United States kept the promise that President Roosevelt made in his speech of December 8—to "win

During the war, women went to work in record numbers at war materials factories and defense plants.

...we here highly resolve that these dead shall not have died in vain...

REMEMBER DEC. 7th!

through to absolute victory.'' In uniform and in worker's garb,
they joined the people of the Allied nations (including Great
Britain and the Soviet Union) in a struggle that would finally
end with the Axis Powers in total collapse.

But that final collapse lay more than three years away.
As 1941 drew to a close, the United States, as we shall see
in the next book in this series, still faced many struggles
before the war would begin to turn in its favor.

BIBLIOGRAPHY

Associated Press. *World War II: A 50th Anniversary History*. New York: Holt, 1989.

Burke, Merle. *United States History: The Growth of Our Land*. Chicago: American Technical Society, 1957.

Devereux, James. *The Story of Wake Island*. Philadelphia: Lippincott, 1947.

Gilbert, Martin. *The Second World War: A Complete History*. New York: Holt, 1989.

Hall, John Whitney, ed. *History of the World: World War I to the Present Day*. Greenwich, Connecticut: Bison Books, 1988.

Lawson, Don. *The United States in World War II*. New York: Abelard-Schuman, 1963.

Millis, Walter. *This is Pearl! The United States and Japan*. New York: Morrow, 1947.

Prange, Gordon W., with Donald M. Goldstein and Katherine V. Dillon. *Dec. 7, 1941: The Day the Japanese Attacked Pearl Harbor*. New York: Warner Books, 1988.

Shapiro, William E. *Turning Points of World War II: Pearl Harbor*. New York: Franklin Watts, 1984.

Steinberg, Rafael, and the editors of Time-Life Books. *Return to the Philippines*. Alexandria, Virginia: Time-Life Books, 1979.

Sulzberger, C. L. *The American Heritage Picture History of World War II*. New York: American Heritage Publishing, 1966.

Toland, John. *But Not in Shame: The Six Months After Pearl Harbor*. New York: Random House, 1961.

_____. *The Rising Sun: The Decline and Fall of the Japanese Empire, 1936–1945*. New York: Random House, 1970.

Zich, Arthur, and the editors of Time-Life Books. *World War II: The Rising Sun*. Alexandria, Virginia: Time-Life Books, 1977.

INDEX